www.buildingleadersseries.com

A MUST FOR JR COLLEGE AND HIGH
SCHOOL STUDENTS & ATHLETES

BUILDING LEADERS
EMPOWERING
STUDENTS & ATHLETES

MARTIN ESQUEDA

*This book will change
your life if you allow it.*

To Carrie

My wife, my business partner, my inspiration

ABOUT COACH MARTIN

As a leadership guru and a black belt in sales, Coach Martin has spoken to over 100 businesses, conferences, and schools nationwide. Coach Martin has also sat on panels with some of the largest financial institutions in the nation.

One of his superpowers is the power to help students and athletes become the leaders they were created to be.

Coach Martin and his wife, Carrie, founded the 501(c)(3) non-profit Time 2 Tell.

TIME 2 Tell hosts free summer camps for kids who have fallen victim to bullying or sexual abuse.

To learn more about Time 2 Tell, visit www.time2tell.org.

CONTENTS

As my mentor always said, you're right whether you think you can or can't. I pray that this book's contents will inspire you to think, act, and become the Leader God created you to be.

HOW TO APPROACH THIS BOOK

I wrote this book for students and athletes. You've come to the right place if you're an athlete looking to get a college scholarship or a student looking to build leadership qualities. ***Building Leaders, Empowering Students & Athletes*** is filled with helpful lessons and interactive resources to help students or athletes at a four-year college, university, community college, high school, or middle school achieve their goals.

Leadership and college recruitment go hand in hand, and the leadership lessons you learn in this book will allow you to go further and impact more people long after the whistle stops. A marathon runner was asked what the secret to finishing his 26.2 miles race was. His answer was ***straightforward— one step at a time.***

So, congratulations on picking up this book, and remember to attack the sections, chapters, and exercises in this book the same way:

One step at a time.

SECTION I

FIVE CHAPTERS THAT BUILD THE FRAMEWORK OF YOUR LEADERSHIP

Get Mentors

Communication

Competence

Commitment

Intentionality

Attitude of Gratitude

WARM-UP BUILDING LEADERS

This book is split into two sections, with the first focusing on leadership and the second concentrating on college recruitment. As in life, there is a crossover between leadership and recruitment; this book is no different. The leadership lessons you'll learn in this book will last a lifetime. Imagine being able to positively IMPACT your friends, family, circles, work, customers, community, and world. Imagine being able to break generational curses. Imagine lives getting changed because their paths happened to cross yours. Exciting, right?

God raises leaders to help accomplish His goals. He doesn't have to, but He partners with his kids. So, are you ready? Are you prepared to lead? Are you ready to build your leadership muscles today? Are you prepared to be used in a mighty way to IMPACT people? I believe you are.

FOR BULK ORDERS

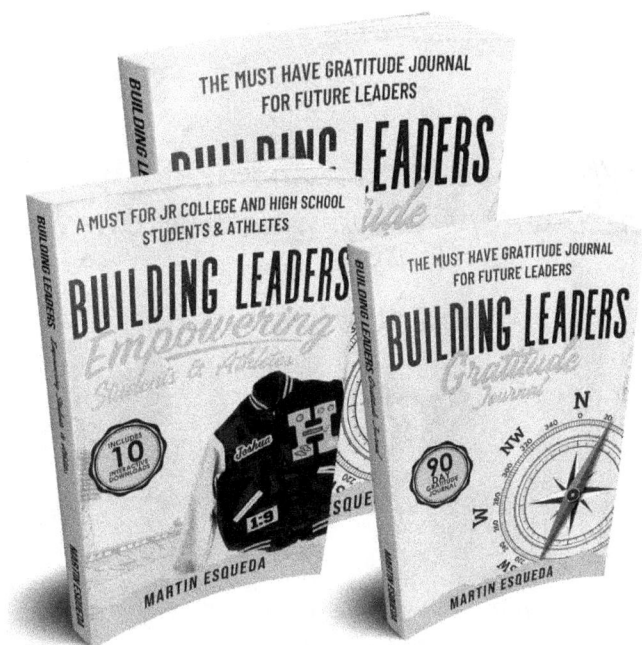

To order bulk, visit www.buildingleadersseries.com
or email info@martinesqueda.com

66

"When a flower doesn't bloom, you fix the environment in which it grows, not the flower."
-Alexander Den Heijer

CHAPTER 1

BUILDING YOUR ENVIRONMENT

*"When a flower doesn't bloom, you fix the environment
in which it grows, not the flower."*
-Alexander Den Heijer

ON YOUR MARK:

Most of us have heard the creation story. God created the world in six days and rested on the seventh day. What most people miss when they read over these first 27 verses in Genesis is that before God created man on the sixth day, He created an ENVIRONMENT so that man could thrive. You see, God knew that having the right environment was crucial for growth and success.

In this chapter, I will lay out the steps necessary to create your winning environment so that you can start your journey of becoming the Leader that God created you to be.

GET SET:

There is a strategic reason why I started this book off on the leadership side. Leadership affects all the other areas of our lives. Leadership affects all the people in our lives. Leadership affects everything. Let me start by giving you some perspective on how leadership affects our daily lives. I will begin with school:

- **A survey finds over 90% of Americans believe students are more successful in school when they can practice leadership outside the classroom.**

(Published December 5, 2017, LEAD4CHANGE)

Now let's look at college recruitment, and let me share with you what I have learned from the college coaches I know.

- **College coaches recruit leaders.**

- **College coaches play leaders.**

- **College coaches trust their leaders when the game is on the line.**

Now let's look at business. Let me share what I have learned from spending years in the private sector. I have interviewed over a thousand applicants in this space, so I know what I'm talking about.

- **Businesses hire leaders.**

- **Businesses promote leaders.**

- **Leaders make more money.**

Are you starting to see a theme? Leaders bring more value. Leaders solve problems. Leaders inspire people. Leaders IMPACT people. Leaders make a difference. Are you ready to start developing your leadership muscle and becoming the Leader you were created to be? Awesome. One thing that leaders possess that others often don't is perspective. Leaders don't see the glass as half empty but rather half full or even more. Leaders don't live with a victim mentality. Leaders see the world through the lenses of opportunity and solutions. Leaders look for chances to help, lead, and impact. Leaders live life through the eyes of gratitude, which brings us to our first exercise. I want to start developing your attitude of gratitude.

Developing your attitude of gratitude is like developing muscles. It takes work, and the muscles grow stronger over time. I would like you to create an attitude of gratitude, and this journey starts every morning. Take a look at the exercise on the next page. I want you to fill this exercise with three people, things, or events you are grateful for. Two people, things, or events that made you happy the day before. And finally, one person that I want you to seek out and say something encouraging to today. (You can encourage more than one person daily, but this part of the exercise will help develop your intentionality).

As you do this exercise, really think about each thing or person you write down. I want you not just to write it out and move on but feel it. Visualize the three things/people each day that you are grateful for. Relive the feeling of the two things that made you happy the day before. And finally, think about who will be that person you will seek out today to encourage. Visualize walking up to them. Visualize what you will say. Will you give them a high five afterward? It would help if you tried to tie a positive emotion behind all six lines. The visualization and feelings connected to this exercise are like weights added to a workout. The more "weights added," the more vital they shape your gratitude perspective. The more days you do this, the faster they shape your gratitude perspective. You get my point.

"Develop your attitude of gratitude today."

GO:

Complete the sample Gratitude List on the next page. It would be best if you completed all of the steps. Making these lists every day will help develop your gratitude, shape your perspective, and build your intentionality. Gratitude is the very foundation of leadership, so start building yours today.

Now that you have some clarity on building your foundation for leadership, be sure to scan the QR code at the end of this chapter, print out copies of your Gratitude List and add this to your morning routine each day. We also have a Building Leaders Gratitude Journal that you can purchase at the end of this book.

"Gratitude is the environment where everything grows."

MY GRATITUDE LIST

I AM thankful for:

_____

_____

_____

Made me happy yesterday:

_____

_____

Today, I will reach out and encourage:

_____

MY GRATITUDE LIST

66

trait
noun
a distinguishing quality (as of personal
character)
Merriam-Webster Dictionary.

CHAPTER

2

BUILDING YOUR TRAITS

trait
noun
a distinguishing quality (as of personal character)
Merriam-Webster Dictionary.

ON YOUR MARK:

When I was a little kid, my favorite television show was Davey and Goliath. I loved that show and watched it every morning before I took the bus to school. Although this show was about a boy and his dog, it took their names directly from the Bible. Most people in our culture have heard the story of David and Goliath at least once. Here is a quick recap if you have never listened to the story. Goliath was the ultimate giant, and David was the ultimate underdog. Most people believe David was just an undersized teenager, about thirteen years old, when he fought the giant, who many believe was over 8' tall.

The truth about the story is that David was so much more than the boy who conquered the giant. He was the boy who became a King, and not only a king but one of the greatest kings that have ever ruled. In this chapter, you will learn how to develop the same two essential traits that David possessed that helped him become one of the greatest leaders ever.

GET SET:

Now it's time to learn about two of David's essential traits, **Commitment & Competence**. These are the building blocks of every great Leader. The first one I want to talk about is COMMITMENT. Without COMMITMENT, nothing else matters. COMMITMENT is necessary for something great to get done. You see, commitment is the key that unlocks everything else, and the good news is that you can generate commitment from within yourself rather than relying on others or luck.

Commitment:

Growing up, David was COMMITTED to spending time with God and tending his sheep. You see, David was a shepherd and was COMMITTED to that role and his relationship with God. David was so COMMITTED that when a lion or a bear took one of his sheep, he would go after it, fight the beast, and bring his sheep back to the flock. There is no way that anybody who is not 100% COMMITTED to their sheep would ever fight a lion or bear to bring it back to safety. NO WAY! Not David; he was committed.

Now, follow me because here is where the story gets good. When the giant Goliath came on the scene, the Bible said that Israel was terrified and nobody would fight the giant, including David's older and bigger brothers. Goliath would walk out onto the battlefield every morning and night, looking for someone to fight. He was the ultimate bully. He did this for 40 days, with not even one person rising to the challenge to fight.

Then one day, David's dad had him take some food to his brothers and bring back news on what was happening on the battlefield. When David went to the battlefield, he saw the giant bullying everyone, so David decided he would take action and fight Goliath. David goes on to fight the giant, and with five rocks, his trusty slingshot, and his faith in God, he takes the giant down. After this, David became a king, a legend, and ultimately one of the greatest leaders the world has ever seen.

Competent:

Many of us skip over this 2nd trait, the competence trait. David was committed to the cause and committed to becoming skilled in fighting, especially with his sling. He became an expert with a rock and his slingshot, and because of this, he became equipped to fight the lion and the bear when they took one of his sheep.

I also imagine that his training was daily. This training allowed him to be prepared and ready when the time presented itself to fight the giant. And as we say... "the rest is history."

I believe that God can do anything he wants to, but He chooses to partner with His kids to accomplish mighty things, just like David. We need to prepare ourselves in certain areas so He can use those things we develop to make history.

Committed & Competent

We need to be committed to becoming a leader and be committed to becoming competent. You can say that we need to become a "black belt" in the areas and roles God has placed us.

If you're a wide receiver on the football team, become a "black belt" at that position by learning the plays like the back of your hand. This way, you can start helping and leading your teammates when they need help.

If you're a point guard on the basketball team, become a "black belt" at learning the plays like the back of your hand. This way, you can start helping and leading your teammates when they need help.

If you work at a restaurant, become a "black belt" by learning everything the job requires, like the back of your hand, so you can start helping and leading your co-workers.

Are you getting my point? Be committed to becoming the Leader that God's calling you to be and be committed to becoming competent at whatever place you find yourself. These two traits are building blocks for leadership.

GO:

I want you to remember that every great Leader, like David, was told hundreds of times that they weren't good enough or weren't qualified. Let me tell you right now that YOU ARE GOOD ENOUGH, and YOU ARE QUALIFIED. If you have a pulse, you have a purpose, and your Purpose is to LEAD!!! If you're ready to step up to the challenge, scan the QR code on the next page, print it out, sign it, and hang it up so you see it daily.

Believe it and declare it out loud daily. You were put here to LEAD!

LEADERSHIP CERTIFICATE

"

"Leadership is a way of thinking, a way of acting, and most importantly, a way of communication."
~Simon Sinek

CHAPTER

3

BUILDING YOUR COMMUNICATION

"Leadership is a way of thinking, a way of acting, and most importantly, a way of communication."
~Simon Sinek

ON YOUR MARK:

I remember watching a video of a college coach discussing scouting a particular athlete. The coach mentioned that even though the athlete was a high-level recruit, the coach wanted to visit one of the player's home games, but here was the twist. The coach secretly saw one of the games the team was supposed to win easily. The reason for visiting this particular game, where this potential recruit probably would only get a little playing time, was to see how the recruit acted on the bench. How did the athlete **communicate** and interact with their teammates? How was the athlete's body language while on the bench? How did the athlete interact and **communicate** with family and friends after the game?

GET SET:

Our words, body language, and actions communicate as athletes or anybody. Leadership is no different. We have to master all three if we want to become effective. Below are a few practical tips to help us in all three areas.

OUR WORDS
OUR BODY LANGUAGE
OUR ACTIONS

OUR WORDS

We should get good at communicating our words. If we are going to lead, we need to get good at clearly conveying our message. We have to get good at passing on instruction in a way that's clear and to the point. How can we lead if someone needs help understanding what we are saying? How can we lead if our messages are mixed? Even if you believe you don't have an issue in this area, everyone can improve from where they're currently at.

At the end of this chapter, we've placed an exercise to help you improve your communication, whatever your current level.

OUR BODY LANGUAGE

Our body language is critical because negative body language can disqualify us and counteract anything positive that we say. Poor body language would have disqualified the recruit above from getting an offer from that coach. Below are some tips on how to improve your body language.

STAND TALL
We convey confidence and authority when we stand tall.

MAKE EYE CONTACT

Eye contact is one of the easiest and most powerful ways to make a person feel recognized, understood, and validated.

SMILE

A genuine smile conveys a sense of warmth and communicates that we care.

SHOW THAT YOU'RE LISTENING

When talking with someone, could you give them our undivided attention? Doing this will convey to them that you are present and care.

OUR ACTIONS

Last but not least is our actions. We can't just talk the talk; we need to walk the walk. I always say a quote to my kids, "Time and money are the great exposers." This means that no matter what someone says or believes, money and time will expose them as genuine or fraudulent. Make sure you walk the walk. James 2:26 says, "For as the body without the spirit is dead, **so faith without works is dead also.**" This is a powerful verse because it tells us that we have to walk the walk. Leadership is no different. Be a leader in your words. Be a leader in your body language. Be a leader before and after the whistle, regardless of the score. But above all, be a leader in your actions.

GO:

Are you ready to develop your communication skills? Whatever your level of communication is, this exercise will elevate it. There is a QR code at the end of this chapter. This QR code will help you develop your communication. Be sure to follow the instructions below and practice this weekly.

Instructions:

1. Scan the QR code and print out the picture.

2. Choose at least one person each week with whom to perform this exercise.

3. You need to describe the entire picture and have them draw it out on paper based only on your verbal instructions.

Here are a couple of rules:

1. They can only see your picture when the exercise is completed.

2. You can only see their drawing when the exercise is completed.

Once this exercise is completed, place both pictures next to each other and see how similar they look. The more you practice this, the more precise your instructions will become, the more similar the pictures will look, and the better your communication skills will become.

"Dream Big, Start Small, But Most Of All, START"
~Simon Sinek

COMMUNICATION SHEET

66

"THE MUST-HAVE RULE...
Find your mentors."

CHAPTER

4

BUILDING YOUR MENTOR LIST

"THE MUST-HAVE RULE...Find your mentors."

ON YOUR MARK:

My wife and I have a signature Bible verse we apply to everything. The verse is Joshua 1:9, which says, Have I not commanded you? Be strong and of good courage; do not be afraid, nor be dismayed, for the Lord your God is with you wherever you go."

Let me set the stage in case you need to become more familiar with the story. Joshua's mentor, Moses, just died, and now God is getting ready to use Joshua to lead His people into the promised land. Joshua 1:9 was a reminder to Joshua not to be afraid during this task because God would be with him every step of the way. God used one Leader, Moses, to mentor and build up another leader, Joshua, to lead the people into the promised land, or across the finish line, as I call it. It took a strong leader to accomplish what God set out, and Joshua was up for the task. He had been mentored and prepared and was now ready to lead.

GET SET:

Everyone does better with a mentor. Mentors help us get better. Mentors help us be better. Mentors help us go farther. Mentors help us to see the blind spots that are all around us. Mentors help us cross the finish lines in our life. I have mentors from whom I gain wisdom daily, weekly, and monthly. One of my weekly mentors is James Malinchak, who was on the ABC hit show Secret Millionaire. I even have a book-writing mentor, Weston Lyon, who was inspirational in my completion of this book. It would help if you had mentors. You can even have mentors, like Weston, who you choose because they can help you in specific areas of your life.

Now I will give you some friendly advice on helping you select your mentors. BE SELECTIVE. Why? Because your mentors will be some of the biggest influences in your life. They can lift and empower you or help cement you right where you are. Use wisdom and caution when selecting them. I have a couple of disqualifiers in place that I use to eliminate people from my mentor list. I call the following two items my **non-negotiables**. Non-negotiables mean not being open to debate.

It would be best if you always had non-negotiables set up in different areas of your life to help you ensure success. Below are my two non-negotiables that will instantly disqualify potential mentors.

NON-NEGOTIABLES:

- **Complainers:**

- **Low Moral Compass:**

Complainers:

If someone is always complaining about something or some-one, I do not want that person as my mentor. Why? Leaders don't complain. Leaders don't criticize. Leaders lead. Leaders focus on solutions, not problems. Leaders always see the glass as full and always full. I always think of one story in Numbers 13:25-14:10. Moses sent ten men to spy out the land and bring back a report. When they returned, eight of the men came back scared and complaining. They were frightened because they focused on the problem. They complained because they were not leaders. Do you get my point?

Meanwhile, only two men, Joshua (from the beginning of this chapter) and Caleb, returned and gave a good report. They didn't complain like the others because they focused on the positive. That's what leaders do. Coach, did Joshua and Caleb see the same land and the same challenges as the other eight? Of course, they did; nevertheless, they believed God would handle all the heavy lifting. It's never about the situation; it's about the story you attach to that situation that ultimate-ly matters. Joshua and Caleb's *story* or *perspective* was that GOD would handle all the obstacles.

Let this example be a good lesson to learn when picking mentors. Many people don't lead because they never devel-oped their leadership muscle. And trust me when I tell you that most people would be happy with you staying anchored right where you're at instead of soaring to new heights. Pick men-tors like Joshua and Caleb, and different from the other eight.

Moral Compass:

When picking mentors, you should discern "by evidence" that your potential mentor is honorable with good character. The apostle Paul lists items a leader should possess in 1 Timothy 3:2-3. To break it down, a leader should have a **good reputa-tion, be faithful, self-controlled, respectable, hospitable, and skilled in teaching**. You can't be leadership-rich and morally bankrupt. Set your bar high, especially in this area. People will rise or fall to the level of expectation you place on them, so when it comes to morality, have high expectations for your mentors. If your mentor is not moral or has low character, how can you trust them to be honest with you? How can you ever trust them to have your best interests in mind? How can you ever trust them to commit to you and the process? The answer is YOU CAN'T.

So be sure you pick your mentors with a solid moral compass.

One of my mentors always says to keep your head high and your standards even higher.

GO:

Scan the QR code at the end of this chapter. Please print out your Mentor Sheet and start filing it in. Your mentors will change over time but start the habit of assigning your mentors and learning from those mentors now. Even if you've never met potential mentors, that shouldn't stop you from reading their books or watching their training classes.

Leaders in Purpose is a faith-based mentorship program that I run. This program has three groups to choose from (high school, middle school, and grade school). I added information about it at the end of this chapter and this book.

"BECAUSE EVERYONE GOES FARTHER WITH A MENTOR"

MENTOR LIST

LEADERS
IN PURPOSE

LEADERS in PURPOSE is our faith-based mentorship program for students and athletes everywhere. Coach Martin and Carrie lead this monthly training to help build their **LEADERSHIP** muscles, prepare them to walk in **PURPOSE**, and help them **IMPACT** the world.

*"BECAUSE EVERYONE GOES
FARTHER WITH A MENTOR"*

www.leadersinpurpose.com

"

*"We all move in the
direction of our thoughts."*

CHAPTER

5

OVERTIME

"We all move in the direction of our thoughts."

Let me share with you my final thoughts on the topic of LEAD-ERSHIP. Everyone reading this book was created with a DIVINE PURPOSE. You were born for something extraordinary and not mediocrity. You were not born to live like a hamster running on a wheel, never gaining ground, never taking territory, and never making a difference. God has called us to live a life of GREATNESS and to IMPACT people along the way.

Please take a look at the three leadership truths I have placed below. Memorize them and let them become the benchmarks for your leadership truth.

Your Purpose predates your conception.
Your Purpose was planned without your input.
Your Purpose doesn't change in a storm.

The truth is, none of the above three will matter if YOU don't be-lieve. YOU have to believe. Everything starts there. If you lack Belief, then borrow someone else's Belief. Just choose this day to **BELIEVE.**

LEADERSHIP is not about you, but it starts with you.

SECTION II

FIVE CHAPTERS TO HELP YOU GET RECRUITED

WARM-UP EMPOWERING STUDENTS & ATHLETES

As founder and CEO of Haystack Sports, I provide cutting-edge software to student-athletes to help empower and streamline their college recruiting journey. While using better software makes the college recruiting QUEST much more manageable, it is in no way a prerequisite. In this section, I will be teaching you the same winning steps I have shared with coaches and student-athletes, like you, all over the country.

Most student-athletes are on the recruitment bench rather than in the recruitment game. Why? Because of inaction. Most of us want things but are unwilling to do what it takes to get them. So, learn the lessons, practice the lessons, and incorporate the lessons. And by doing so, you will get off that recruitment bench and give yourself a fighting chance to win that college scholarship.

"Discipline is the bridge between goals and accomplishments."
~Jim Rohn

66

"You cannot make progress without making decisions."
~Jim Rohn

CHAPTER 6

BUILDING YOUR YES

"You cannot make progress without making decisions."
~Jim Rohn

ON YOUR MARK:

A statistic once said that when a student-athlete goes unrecruited, over 50% of those athletes and their parents blame the coach, the school, or both. If this statistic is accurate, it tells me that 50% of the student-athletes we just mentioned never BUILT their YES. What does that mean, coach? Let me explain. They never decided to be all in. They never committed to the process. They never chose to take responsibility for their college recruitment. You see, *everything* starts with a decision. Jim Rohn once said: *"You cannot make progress without making decisions."*

GET SET:

The Indecision Road:

Let's talk briefly about the INDECISION ROAD that 50% above walked on. This road starts with someone not deciding something -- this could be anything. Because we never chose to be committed, we wouldn't have to take responsibility for accomplishing it. Next, not taking responsibility for something frees us up from all accountability. If we are free from accountability, we no longer have to do the work required to accomplish our goal. Finally, if we don't do the work needed to achieve our goals, we will never get the result we hoped for in the beginning. Do you see how the chain reaction works? I call this the road to nowhere.

NO DECISION leads to **NO RESPONSIBILITY,** which leads to **NO ACCOUNTABILITY,** which leads to **NO WORK,** which leads to **NO RESULTS.**

Go ahead and complete the
crossword puzzle on the next page.

Limiting Beliefs:

The next thing I want to address is limiting beliefs. All of us have limiting beliefs running around in our heads. What is a limiting belief? A limiting belief is a thought or state of mind that we take as truth and stops us from doing certain things. A limiting belief tells us we can't do something because of **(fill in the blank)**.

Limiting beliefs can come from anywhere, from our parents, teachers, friends, movie stars, professional athletes, etc. Imagine if the Wright Brothers gave up when people told them they could never fly. Imagine if Thomas Edison listened to the doubters and gave up and never invented the light bulb. Imagine if Rudy listened to his family and all the other doubters about him going to Notre Dame and playing on their football team.

The main point I want you to get is that it doesn't matter what anyone else thinks you can or can't do. The ONLY thing that matters is, do you believe. Do YOU think that there is a college out there that wants you? Do YOU believe that you got what it takes? If your answer was yes, then CONGRATULATIONS. If your answer was no, borrow someone else's Belief, and let's get to it.

One of my mentors, Megan Unsworth, has an excellent saying for limiting beliefs that she has copyrighted. She says you have to CATCH IT, CANCEL IT, and then REFRAME IT. An example would be to write down your limiting Belief (CATCH IT), cross it out (CANCEL IT), and then REFRAME it by writing down why you can accomplish it. I want you to commit this to memory. Commit to internalizing this so it becomes like the birthday song. At the end of this chapter, you can try this yourself. After you have done this example, please focus on the reframed Belief moving forward. Remember, whatever you focus on expands, so focus only on the reframe. I have done this with one of my limiting beliefs below so you can see what I mean.

Coach Martin

Limiting Belief: *I cannot write and publish a book.*

Limiting Belief: *I cannot write and publish a book. (Please cross this line out)*

Reframed Belief: *"I can do all this through HIM, who strengthens me."*

Do you see how this works? Be sure to do this exercise at the end of this chapter. Use this exercise whenever a limiting belief pops up in your head.

"Whatever You Focus on Expands"

Game Plan:

Accomplishing goals is all about **commitment, having the right plan, and putting the right amount of effort into that plan.**

- **COMMITMENT**

- **GAME PLAN**

- **EFFORT**

The other chapters of this book will get into the game plan, but let's focus for a minute on COMMITMENT. You have to decide. You have to commit. You have to be committed to getting a scholarship. You have to be committed to taking 100% responsibility. You have to be committed to doing the work.

If you can do these three things (commit, remove your limiting beliefs, and create your game plan), you can accomplish many goals in your life, starting with recruitment. The rest of this book will help you with that plan.

GO:

Now that we got all that out of the way let's talk about making a decision. Everything starts with a decision. Every dream ever reached first began with the decision to chase it. But coach, what if I fail? Failure is never about coming up short. Failure is ALWAYS in not trying. We only indeed fail in life when we don't try. You see, even when we set a goal and come up short, we always learn something during the process that will set us up and help us with our future goals and plans. Business professionals call this Fail Forward. Do you want to get that college scholarship? Are you committed to doing the work necessary to accomplish this goal? Are you committed to taking 100% responsibility for this mission? If the answer to these three questions was YES, then let me be the first to say CONGRATULATIONS!!!!!

On the next page, there is a limiting belief exercise that I want you to do. In the Limiting Belief section, write GETTING A COLLEGE SCHOLARSHIP. Next, cross it out and finally reframe it with something else, and from now on, I want you to concentrate on the reframe.

Finally, I have added a QR code with a COMMITMENT CERTIFICATE. Be sure to print it out, sign it, and hang it somewhere in your house. Let it be your declaration of commitment.

NAME:

Limiting Belief:

Reframed Belief:

SCHOLARSHIP CERT

CROSSWORD PUZZLE

Puzzle 1

Word bank

ACCOUNTABILITY   DECISION   RESPONSIBILITY   RESULTS   WORK

66

"A team will always outproduce an individual."
~Coach Martin

CHAPTER 7

BUILDING YOUR TEAM

"A team will always outproduce an individual."
Coach Martin

ON YOUR MARK:

One of my favorite movies of all time is Miracle. I've watched it at least ten times. It's a story of a bunch of college kids that beat the Soviet hockey team in the 1980 Olympics. This event is still one of the greatest sports miracles of all time, and in my book, it's still #1.

I will give you a quick recap if you have never seen the movie. The coach for Team USA, Herb Brooks, had to assemble a hockey team full of college players because professional athletes didn't play in the Olympics then. The task was to beat the Soviet hockey team, the most dominant hockey team in the world. Maybe even the greatest ever. The Soviet team was so dominant that they destroyed the NHL All-Star team shortly before. Coach Brooks had to assemble a team with a specific purpose. Each player is selected to fill a role. Some people thought he was crazy, but that didn't stop him. He had a goal, and he had a plan for that goal, and now he needed the right players.

It's now your turn to assemble your gold medal team. Your goal is a college scholarship. Your plan will be laid out over the following two chapters, but now it's time to select your team.

GET SET:

So why do I need a team, and what will they do? Do I have to pay my team? Where will I find them? What if they say no? Okay, let's slow down and take a deep breath. A team will always outproduce an individual, so building your recruitment team is paramount to success. You will select a team around you to help you in your quest for that college scholarship. Below are a few of the positions you should fill.

Accountability Coach:

This person will be assigned the task to help make sure you complete your tasks. Have a check-in call (weekly, bi-monthly, or monthly) with them so they can hold you accountable for what you say you will do. If you tell them you will reach out to ten target colleges this month, they will be the person to keep you responsible.

Another option would be to create a Google Spreadsheet and share this sheet with the accountability coach. This way, you can load your weekly goals and check them off once completed, and your Accountability Coach would be able to see your progress in real-time. Going this route is recommended, but check-in calls are still highly encouraged. Some fields you can add to the Excel sheet would be Target Colleges, Coaches' Names, Coaches' emails, Coaches' Phone Numbers, Coaches' Social Media Handles, Date Contacted, Type of Contact (email, phone, social media), Coaches' Response, etc.

Role Play Coach:

Your role-play coach will be assigned the task of helping prepare you for your phone calls with your target college coaches. You should give this position to a family member or family friend who is in sales if you have one, or you may have a family member who is a real estate agent. Real estate agents would be a good fit for this role since most role-play in their brokerage. Your Role Play Coach will help to prepare you to talk smoothly, ask the right questions, and handle any objections you might receive from the target college coach. You want to sound prepared and polished on your calls, and your Role Play Coach will help you accomplish that goal.

Your Sports Coaches:

This will include your coaches, position coaches, and any professional instructors you have. Meet with them individually and let them know you have set a goal to play at the next level and will target college coaches. Ask them to assess which college level you should be targeting. NCAA DI, DII or DIII? NAIA? Junior College? It is critical to have them evaluate which college level they think you're a good fit for. Log what each coach tells you so you can use their information to help you build your target list. (We will go into this further a little bit later in the book) Ask your coaches if you can check in with them occasionally to ask questions and get some advice on your recruiting journey. Most often, they will appreciate this and say yes.

Guidance Counselor:

Set up a meeting once per year to meet with your guidance counselor. Let them know which college level you will be targeting so they can ensure you are taking the correct classes to qualify for your target colleges. How horrible would it be to get an offer only to be disqualified for not being eligible? Your guidance counselor will help you ensure this never happens to you.

GO:

Teamwork makes the dream work; it's time to start assembling your team. On the next page, scan the QR code and print out your Team Sheet. Please fill it out and leverage your team to help you in your SCHOLARSHIP QUEST.

"You Can't Build Something Great Alone"

66

"Don't wish it was easier;
wish you were better."
~Jim Rohn

CHAPTER

8

BUILDING YOUR PROFILE & LIST

"Don't wish it was easier; wish you were better."
~Jim Rohn

ON YOUR MARK:

Think about everything for a minute that is around you right now. I have a desk, chair, television, clock, computer, etc. Write down five items that are around you right now.

1. _____

2. _____

3. _____

4. _____

5. _____

Now take a look at everything that you wrote down. The visual I want you to get is that somebody built those items. To BUILD means *ACTION taken to create something.* You see, God is a builder and has called us to be builders. Now it's your time to BUILD. This chapter will *teach you how to BUILD* your recruiting profile and target college list.

GET SET:

Your recruiting profile, target college list, and contact with college coaches are the three pivotal pieces to the college recruiting process. Most student-athletes get at least one of these wrong (if not all) and derail their scholarship quest by doing so.

Let's start with the first pivotal piece—recruiting profile. Most athletes leave off valuable information, or they EXAGGERATE. Exaggerations are lies and directly attest to your character. Whatever you do, don't lie. Good leaders don't lie. Below is the information for you to BUILD your recruiting profile.

#1 RECRUITING PROFILE:

There are a lot of creative ways to BUILD your recruiting profile. Registering on websites like Haystack Sports allows you to BUILD a digital recruiting profile. You can also build a "one sheet" from a Word document and add this to your emails. At the end of this chapter, I have added a QR code with an example of a digital resume, so you can see what I'm talking about. If you build a "one sheet," incorporate the sections below. Whichever route you go, make sure of two things:

1. You have access to complete control of your recruiting profile. That means that "you" can send it to whoever you want, whenever you want.

2. Ensure you include the below sections in your recruiting profile.

RECRUITING PROFILE SECTIONS:

PHOTO: Add a picture of you where they can see your face.

ABOUT ME: Share a little information about you.

MY ACCOMPLISHMENTS: List your athletic and academic accomplishments here. Also, list other awards you might have won outside of the athletic realm.

METRICS: This is where you will add your age, height, weight, gender, and dominant hand/foot.

SPORT: Add your primary sport and position and any other sports you play.

ACADEMICS: Add your high school, city, state, graduation year, GPA, SAT/ACT scores, desired college major, and NCAA/NAIA eligibility numbers (if applicable).

PARENT/GUARDIAN INFORMATION: Add the first name, last name, phone number, email, and relationship to you.

COACHES/PROFESSIONAL INSTRUCTORS INFORMATION: Add the first name, last name, email, phone number, sport, and instructor type (Examples: High School, Private, Club, etc.)

STATISTICS: Add your statistics to the primary sport you play. (Keep these updated)

VIDEOS: Video is a must because it's one of the main ways a college coach evaluates a potential recruit. Your video showcases your abilities and should reflect that. Your videos should cover three main areas.

HIGHLIGHTS... SKILLS... PERSONAL

Highlight Video: This video should cover highlights in your game settings that will grab the coaches' attention. This video should be between 3-5 minutes.

Skills Video: Your skills video should be footage outside the game settings. This video should focus on the skills that your target coach would be interested in. This video should be 1-3 minutes.

Personal Video: This should be a short video of you sharing a quick blurb about you and your commitment. Talk to the camera like you would be talking to the coach. This video should be between 20-60 seconds.

Now that you have the ingredients for your Recruiting Profile, I have one more thing to add, DON'T OVERTHINK IT. **Procrastination is the enemy of progress,** so gather the ingredients above and BUILD that profile! You can always make adjustments down the road, but today isn't that day. Today is the day to BUILD.

#2 TARGET SCHOOLS:

Now let's address the second pivotal piece: selecting the right target schools. I cannot stress how important this task is. Most student-athletes get this wrong; nothing else you do will matter if this part is wrong. You have to get this right. That's why we added our coaches to our team in Chapter 2, so they can help us get this right. Review all the information your coaches gave you and start Building your Target List. This list should include three types of schools:

STRETCH SCHOOLS: This is a list of schools *slightly* above our CURRENT athletic and academic abilities.

TARGET SCHOOLS: This is a list of schools that fit our CURRENT athletic and academic abilities.

FALL-BACK SCHOOLS: This is a list of schools slightly below our CURRENT athletic and academic abilities.

The rule of thumb for these should be 10% of your target schools should be your STRETCH SCHOOLS, 70% should be your TARGET SCHOOLS, and 20% should be your FALL-BACK SCHOOLS.

10/70/20

GO:

Now that you have the plan for your profile and target schools, scan the QR code on the next page. You can print out and fill in your Target College List based on the model above. Be sure to print out as many pages as needed based on the size of your overall list. In business, we use the term, WHATEVER YOU TRACK AND MEASURE IMPROVES. So, be sure you track and measure your progress today by using your Target College List.

TARGET COLLEGE SHEET

RECRUITMENT PROFILE

RECRUITMENT PROFILE by HAYSTACK SPORTS.
To get a digital profile, visit www.haystacksports.com

66

"College recruitment is a contact sport."
Coach Martin

CHAPTER 9

BUILDING YOUR CONTACT

"College recruitment is a contact sport."
Coach Martin

ON YOUR MARK:

One lasting memory happened during my first year at football practice. During this practice, our coach performed a drill where he would call two players out to face off against each other in a three-point stance just a few feet apart. At the sound of the whistle, these two players would fire off against each other and try to drive the other player back. I will never forget what happened next. One particular time, one of the two players called to face off was much larger than the other. When the coach blew the whistle, the much smaller player fired off first and initiated the hit.

The coach stopped the drill and yelled to the bigger kid, "ARE YOU THE HAMMER or THE NAIL?" The bigger kid responded, probably without much thought, "THE NAIL." He didn't mean to say that; it slipped out, but you could imagine the laughter.

My point to this story is that college recruitment is a CONTACT SPORT. You cannot be the nail because being the nail will not get you recruited. You have to be the hammer. You must be able to contact and talk with college coaches on your target list. The rest of the chapter will help you with that.

GET SET:

One of the hardest and scariest things to do is to pick up the phone and call a target coach, especially one who doesn't know who you are. Trust me when I tell you that I have coached and trained thousands of sales professionals, most of whom share the same feelings as you. So why do we get scared and nervous about calling a stranger and pitching our product or services? The answer is simple: NOBODY LIKES REJECTION. It's this fear of being rejected that will overwhelm us "IF" we let it. The good news is I will teach you how to overcome the fear and start conversing with the very coaches with the power and authority to give you the scholarship. Are you ready?

FIRST, THE MINDSHIFT: You have to come to a place of being comfortable being uncomfortable; this is the breeding ground for growth. Think about it for a minute. If we only did something once, we were good at it; we would never start. Why? Because we were never comfortable, to begin with. Comfort comes as we get better. And, to get better, we have to do it. Please don't say to yourself that you will do it later. Sometimes later becomes never, so do it now!

NOW THE TOOLS: Return to the TEAM SHEET you printed in Chapter 7. Now it's time to utilize one of your team members, your role-play partner. Your role-play partner will help you prepare and become a "black belt" on phone calls with your target coaches. Set up one day a week to call them on your phone and practice role-playing the conversation. They will be the coach, and you will be you. The conversation might sound bad the first few times you do it, but keep going. The more you practice, the better you become. The better you become, the more impressed your target coach will be when they get off the phone with you. Before you know it, you will be a ninja on the phone. Now let's go a little deeper for a minute. This skill that you're developing will stay with you forever. It carries over to your future job interviews. It carries over to your future job promotions. It will pay dividends for the rest of your life.

PLAYBOOK: Always start with an email and follow up with a phone call. Email your target coach, letting them know about your interest in their program. Go ahead and add a little information about yourself. Email them again if you have not received a reply after a week. If you haven't received a response this second time, it's time for the call. I have added a sample email on the next page that you can use as a template. Always remember that college recruitment is not a sideline sport. It's a player's sport; to win your college scholarship, you must be active. I have added an email template at the end of this chapter that you can use as a guide.

BONUS: Exposure is critical to getting recruited. The more coaches know about you, the better your chances of getting recruited. Sometimes student-athletes attend showcases and camps where college coaches will be. The problem with most athletes is that they attend camps and showcases where the participating colleges are not on their target lists. The other issue is that athletes attend these events like everyone else, hoping to stand out. Friends, hope is not a strategy. My tip is to show up differently from everyone else. Find out what colleges will be present at the event. Contact those colleges and determine which coaches will be present at the event. Next, contact those particular coaches, introduce yourself and set up a one-minute meet and greet with them at the event. This step alone will separate you from the others and allow you to start a connection. You can use the same process as above.

*If all of the target colleges are outside of your target group, then consider placing your energy in other areas that can be fruitful.

GO:

Take a look at the sample email template on the next page. Feel free to use it as your guide. You can also scan the QR code and download the College Script Book. Memorize, internalize, and practice on your calls with your role-play coach.

COLLEGE COACHES
EMAIL TEMPLATE

COLLEGE COACHES
SCRIPT BOOK

66

*"It takes a giant **why** to outlast a giant obstacle."*
~Coach Martin

CHAPTER
10

2ND OVERTIME

*"It takes a giant **why** to outlast a giant obstacle."*
~Coach Martin

I've been asked this question repeatedly by many parents, coaches, and athletes. Is there a college out there for any student-athlete who wants to get recruited? My answer is always the same, YES, If the student-athlete can answer YES to my following three questions.

Are you targeting the right schools based on your athletic and academic levels?

Are you contacting coaches and doing the work required to land a college scholarship?

What is your WHY, and is it BIG enough?

The first two questions are pretty straightforward, but it's always the third one they have to think about. What is your WHY?

Your WHY is your PURPOSE for doing or accomplishing a particular task or item.

Think about WHY you want that college scholarship and write it down at the end of this chapter.

Please commit to memorizing your WHY. Remember your WHY. Commit to learning it and having it become part of your everyday life. When all else fails, REMEMBER YOUR WHY. When things start to get complicated, REMEMBER YOUR WHY. Whenever you feel like quitting, REMEMBER YOUR WHY. We all should have a WHY. It's the WHY that keeps us going long after everybody else stops. When David

fought Goliath, he had a WHY. When Nehemiah BUILT the wall, he had a WHY. When Joshua went into battle, he had a WHY. One day someone will share your recruiting journey with others, and they will tell them about your WHY.

Congratulations on finishing this book. Be sure to commit to all the steps in this book. Remember that discipline is truly the bridge between goals and accomplishments. So become disciplined in everything you do, and watch as there will be nothing you cannot accomplish.

Everything in life that is worth wanting will require you to take a risk to get it.
~Keith A. Craft

WRITE YOUR "**WHY**" FOR GETTING RECRUITED

"ONLY A GIANT WHY WILL OUTLAST
YOUR GIANT OBSTACLES."

In everything you do, have a WHY.

STAY CONNECTED

🌐 www.martinesqueda.com

📷 @officialcoachmartin

in @martinesqueda

🐦 @martinesqueda

✉ info@martinesqueda.com

BOOK COACH MARTIN TO SPEAK

Request Coach Martin To Speak

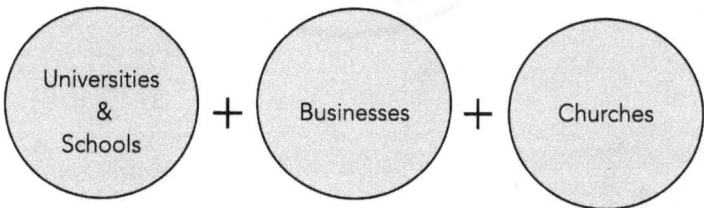

Universities & Schools + Businesses + Churches

For

Leadership events, sales trainings, conferences, and events.

www.martinesqueda.com

ADDITIONAL PRODUCTS & SERVICES FROM COACH MARTIN

http://www.nationalsigningdaypodcast.com/

http://www.buildingleadersseries.com/

http://www.time2tell.org/

http://www.martinesqueda.com/

http://www.haystacksports.com/

LEADERS
IN PURPOSE

LEADERS in PURPOSE
MENTORSHIP PROGRAM

Because everyone goes farther with a mentor

"

"Some people Succeed because they are Destined, but most because they are Determined."
~Unknown